AF407990

A Moment of Thought

And a little bit of envy

Dedication

I dedicate this to the number four. At four am, like clockwork, I would wake up and write what's on my mind. It doesn't always turn into master pieces but it's done me good. I dedicate this work to this brain of mine who decided to keep fighting on, even when she wanted to give into the temptations of giving up. I dedicate this book to myself - I am all that I've got really.

To JayJay, I hope you live till the daisy's die - I hope they never die.

To Lexei, I hope you're happy now, I really hope you're happy.

Born into Nothing

The sun bleeds and the moon weeps,
In tune with the crying of a sparrow.
The bellowing babe sings great song
Along with rhyme and rhythm;
Mama gushes with great greed,
Heart torn for the lowly thing.

But, what should be arms of comfort,
It instead shrieks vexation.

Time, it needs more time,
He needs more time.

He needs to feed upon her teat,
To catch a drop of her devotion.
He needs his mothers doting intimacy,
That hand to clasp onto,
That beating heart close to his ear,
The soothing chords of her grand piano.

For this solus creature,
Time is everything.

But time is up.

Without its keeper,
The child seizes to sing,
The sun's rays burn instead of illuminate.
Darkness floods,
The rising tides envelop him.
Leaving the chit with nothing but a numbing hold.

Like father - past and present,
Crisp air is left in her wake,
Blending with the running wind.

Mother is no more.

A child born seeking sanctuary
Was instead granted with a life of solitude-
Zeal and passion knows him not,
But revulsion does.

Mothers are supposed to love like no other,
Their hate smoulders just as intensely.

This I Pray

Strike me down,

Show me mercy

Dear Lord,

Grant me death.

For I am only

worthy of

the end

.

Her

The way she strolls across this planet
She travels so effortlessly

      Her body sways to the winds command
      Her hair sings with the breeze

Those eyes glisten to the stars in the sky
Her soft touch heals my aching wounds

      She is everything to be
      She is the only thing I see

Because she is perfection,
to me.

I've loved, finally, I've loved.

I've lived, I've lost; But I have never loved,
Not until you.

Not until you crossed my path,
The path scattered bomb shells,
Shards spewed from an empty being.

Pieces that I thought had been lost,
You've searched the rising tides to gift them back,
Sat me down and patched me up.
You even kissed each painful wound,
to just an aching memory.

I was happy with you,
We talked, sang to each other's hearts.
We played in the growing daisies,
Frolocked under the pouring clouds.

I've never met anyone like you.

You were my first love,
The first person to ever hold my heart.
The first person to hear it beat in my chest,
The one an only thing that makes me smile each
morning,
        From the rising sun to the setting moon.

Oh, my dear, I love you.

I have lived, and now have lost,
But I have never loved,
Like I loved you.

To you I say goodbye.

For I have loved you till your last breath,
And now,
until mine.

Slaughter

The screams of the fallen
They cry out for mercy
But no mercy granted

The sounds of bones crushing
Teeth grinding

The thudding of the crashing bodies
Echo through the midnight air.

The half-moon sneaks in
This dark cell I call home

The floor, cold to the touch.
The crisp air reveals my breath

Then I hear; footsteps.

They get closer
I feel the vibrations on the floor

My body goes numb
My eyes widen
My jaw clenches
Not releasing a breath.

I hear keys jingle

Locks being opened

The squeals of the taken

I'm next

Off to my doom
Or just to the rest of it.

Meal Ticket

When I think of home,
going back feels like
trying to swim to the surface
while handcuffed to a sinking ship.

The sharks beneath are just waiting
for your head to slip under
one last time,

You can almost hear them
clap with gratitude.

You can feel your surroundings
ripple around you,
their teeth nipping at your heels.

You never last long,
If you last at all.

Battle

The lives of many
Lost on this starlit night

The moon shines upon their shallow graves

The slaughter has begun

Soaked in the tears of my enemies
Their blood stains my clothes

My cup fills with the last breaths of the fallen

The faces engraved on my being for eternity
Their screams forever etched into my memories.

Pleasure

A necklace of purple bruises surround my breath
Paired with a bracelet of red throbbing goodness

The swelling of my bottom lip
share pain with my aching insides

The wax burns make their way up my being
Waking every nerve ending, riding them to its peak

My toes curl at the sensation

I'm sweltering from the inside out

Every touch grows me closer

Barely able to stop the lunge off the edge of this
seemingly never-ending cliff

Dreams

When I was young, I had a dream
A dream that would fix everything

I would grow big and strong
So, I can conquer anything

I would be able to fly super-fast
And run at the speed of light

I would be able to see through walls
And punch out the bad guy

As I grew, my dreams shrunk
The real world started to hit me
The world is broken
I can't fix it

But it seems like it doesn't want fixing

As a child it was fun to think of the future
The older you get, the less hope you have.
Children never give up
I wish I were still a child

Sincerely

A kiss you lay on my fair lips,
A hand you hold, warm and kind

You are mine, and I am yours.

Soft music sings in the background
These precious hands shimmer with diamonds
Forever we last, our hearts join as one.

"I do, I do."

Your body flush against mine
These two souls, written together in the stars.

I take your hand in marriage
We last for eternity, my love.

But,

You think I glow, and my smile genuine
But behind this mask

Tears fall.
The hand I hold,
Is the object to my suffering.

You beat and burn me,
You yell and torment

Your words ring filthily through my head,

I'm swimming in restlessness.

Blood spattered on walls,
The crimson stains mix with my salty tears.

I'm tired of living in a shell,
Forever being tortured.
Being led by you sweet husband,

I am not happy,
I never was.

I can no longer lead this life.

And now to you
I say goodbye,

As the vows did say,
"Till death do us part."
Now death, we part.

Stuck

I'm stuck.

Stuck in forever impenetrable box
Filled to the brim with never ending thoughts.

And it's drowning me.

It's been drowning me for a while now but,
I still seem to keep my head above water.

The crackling of the thunder
and the shock of the lightning
Still make me jump.

But when the storm is over,
the beaming sun shines
a rainbow colours the skyes
and the water stops filling.

I can breathe.
Even though barely,

I can breathe.

Entry 68

under my skin,
in my bones,
you sleep peacefully.

in you,
i lay lovingly.

apart of you
apart of me

as one whole,

longingly looking-

forever.

I wish upon a floating star, please help me wherever you are

Have you ever wished you could just taste the sun?
You could swallow the pungent rays,
You could feel the energy flow through you?

Have you ever wished to swim on the moon?
Of course there isn't actually an ocean there,
But rather, do you wish to float along with its
currents?
To stay atop its highest peak and float to its lowest
valleys.

Have you ever wished to climb the stars?
It would be nice to bask along its blinding colours,
Touch its surface, just to feel its exquisite body
contrast.

Have you ever wished to feel?
Like, really feel?

No matter if it's like the happiness of a playing child

Or the sad mourning of a mother burying her only
brother.

Have you ever wanted something so simple as
feelings,
That it hurts when you can't even have that?
No matter what you do,
No matter the stress and effort you've made,
You will never feel.

All you have is nothing.
There is no tasting the sun or swimming on the
moon.
There is no running with the wind or climbing the
stars.

All that's there
Is you.
You and your lack of humanity.

What makes others truly one with life has passed
you over.
What makes others tick has sent you spiralling.

There is no crawling out of this darkened oceanic
floor,
There is only drowning,

Becoming one with the empty abyss I call hell.

All you have is pain.
But I guess that is the feelings you asked for,
Isn't it?

These feelings I speak of,
It's a weird want of mine it seems.
All my life I've wanted to just stop it all.
Stop the overwhelming thoughts,
The annoying nagging voice.

Some might think it's a simple request, right?
"I just want to be happy!"
Happiness, I've slowly come to find,
Isn't as simple as it seems.

I really do wish I could swim on the moon,
Climb the shiny blue star,
Taste the glowing yellow sun.

I want to feel it,
I want to feel it all.

Deja vu

I've done this before,
I've been just right here.

It's a loop.

One that I wish
someone would hit
the pause button on.

Lemons

They say suck it up

Take what your given
"When life give you lemons, make lemonade"

They taught me what to do to get there
But never what to do when I have arrived

What if the lemonade is too sour?
Did I make too little, or too much?

How many do I use,
some grew too small to juice
Some are all dried out

What happens when I can't make a good batch?

"When life gives you lemons, make lemonade"

But what if life's lemons aren't good enough for a
nice refreshing drink?

Safely

22

I'm tired of

being stuck
trying to
save you

from you.

Eat

Tonight,
We feast.

Make life our own.
Because what is the point otherwise?

Smothering

My love is the ignition
to your flames
      Behind me there is nothing left but

                        ash.

Childlike Wishes

It's sad really.
Children have such a yearning to grow older,
Whether it's because they want just an ounce of
independence
Or because they want to feel in control, even just
for a little while.

It's sad really.
That a lot of adults rather have stayed a child.
Whether that's because they yearn to be taken care
of again,
Or because they are tired of endless responsibility.

It's sad really.
That we humans are stuck with these thoughts.
We have these weird expectations of how life
should be,
It has only ended up disappointing us in the long
run.

We are stuck hoping and wishing for something
different,
Anything really.

Something that can counteract this negative notion
of life,

But so far, our search for something deeper-
Something more
Has driven us into never ending pits of questioning.

When I was a child, I wished to grow up.

I wanted to be my own person-
Make my own decisions
Be a product of my own choices.

And now, as I've grown older,
I realise that no matter what,
I wish to have stayed a child.

As a child, you hoped and dreamed for things to get
better.

But, it turns out,
It's only gotten worse.

I wished to escape a home,
A hellish place.
It seems that I've grown to open a door to even
hotter flames

Rainbows End

Why do people associate thunderstorms with
sadness?
They use words like dreary, panicked, exhausted,
maybe even confused.

Once the storm is over and a rainbow appears,
it's apparently the opposite
The colourful light that reflects off the soft water
beads
brings to light the after effects of a thunderstorm.

It's weird how people associate dread with thunder,
Anger with lightning,
Hurt with the pelting droplets

To me
Storms are like hugs

They are warm, cozy, love filled
Storms for me create the space to be free

It's like the clouds are my eyes
The rain are my tears
The rainbow is my smile

Storms are cathartic
After each one I feel light,
I feel what people describe when they step foot
under the sunny sky

For me, storms mean love, freedom, sanctuary.

The clouds are my sun,
The cold windy chills are my beach breeze
The thunder is my blanket of warmth,
The lightning are my rays of shine.

Storms are a language I had no idea I could speak
A language where I feel at home.

My Star

To you dear,
I say yes.

'Cause there is nothing
I want more
Then to see you shine.

Shine,
oh shine.

Life is death
Letting me live
Is letting me go.

Leave me without thought.

Let me be,
Send me along with nothing
but my own notions.

Leave me to wallow,
Let me sink further
Into the depths of my own
Monstrous doings.

Let me live,
Let me live
by letting me go.

Let me die.

Deadly Love

I never thought that I would find love.
I could never have imagined liking someone more
than myself.

It's funny how I ended up falling for someone
destined to leave me,
destined to destroy.

What we are, well,
what we were,
it's that painful love.

I want to kiss you until your lips bleed,
I want to hug you until your lungs give way.
I want to drive into the depths of the ocean with you
strapped to my middle.

You betrayed me.

You ripped me from what I knew.
You threw me off a cliff,
landing me into this sort of blissful kind of torture.

You hurt me.

You drove your resentment so deep into my chest,
I almost felt sorry for you.

You strung me by my heels
Left me dangling over shark infested water.

I gave you my love,
I gave you all of me,
And you used my trust
And destroyed me.

That's my mistake though.

There is nothing for me here,
But all there is for you,
is me.

That's why you sought to destroy me.
I was the closest thing you had,
the only person to tie you to humanity.

We are the same in a sense.

No matter how hard we tried to be different from
one another.
No matter how many times we left,
We always ended up meeting again.

We were meant to hurt others,
meant to hurt ourselves.

I love you,
but death has your heart.

We did say until the bitter end,
right?

Doubles

Let me belong
Someplace
Else

Someplace
More

Somewhere worth my while.

Let me heal,
Be healed

Love,
Be loved

Let me be

Just let me be.

INFINITY

Contrary to popular belief
Endings don't always have to mean something.

They don't always have to be sad.
Our life doesn't have live by the standards of fairy
tale books
Or miracle stories.

I like to believe that endings open doors
Instead of closing them.

Life and its opposite,
It's an infinite loop of possibility.

So honestly,
Is there ever a true ending?

Only Thing

Kiss me like you're dying.

I want you to think
that this will be it,
that this will be the last time we see one another.

Kiss me like its your last breath,

Love me like
it's the only thing to do.

Because what I am to you,
What you are to me-

We are all that matters.

Loud

It's just the voices, you know?

The ones that riddle with your mind
day in and day out.

They just love to scream your name,
Mark your day with their endless torture.

Mind games I call it,
The irony is almost laughable.

Don't you hate it when they tell you what to do?

Like when your having a nice stroll on the beach
And they tell you to go for a swim.

But you don't know how to swim
Also maybe slightly deathly afraid of the ocean.

Or when you're driving over a bridge,
one slight hand jerk away from eternal damnation.

That last one doesn't seem too bad though.

Only because it seems like things can only get
better from here.

Don't you hate it when you're just going about your
day,
Out of nowhere they scream to bang your head
against anything in sight.

Or to just run into oncoming traffic.

Those days though aren't as bad as the ones where
they're quiet.

Quiet days are the loudest.

Because you know they will come back eventually,
They are lying in wait
Scouting out their prey,
Waiting to pounce at the right moment.

Those are the days all you can do is lay in bed
waiting for the inevitable,

The silence is deafening.
Because it's so loud.

38

Sometimes

Sometimes, just sometimes,
I wish that I were happy.

Or at least anything but sad, or numb.

Having that feeling,
or not feeling,
somehow hurts.

Hurts to the point where all I want is to say
goodbye.

Being numb to everything around you somehow
still finds a deep way to cut you.

Feeling sad and unmovable,
it makes you long for the numb days

Because on those days,
you know what you want,
You want to feel.

So when you actually start to feel,
What then?

What do I do then
With these unmovable days?

Where my feet drag against the cold hard wood
When I rather back get scolded by the fire pellets of
my morning shower.

What should I do?

It's hard wanting to feel and then hating the actual
feelings.

It all just,
hurts.

Sometimes life is an unbreakable curse,
And death can be a great gift.

Gods Will

The devil isn't the one you should be scared of.

The devil has never lied to you.

We know the evil he can ensue.
We know the feeling of his torment.

What hurts is when God takes you for a ride.

And yet its still,
"In God we trust".

Why?

You still say you love me,
Why does your love feel
So hate filled?

Black Dahlia

> Some people are born good,
> > born pure.

How could they not?
You're born with no knowledge,
No understanding of the world around you.

Some are born,

And down the road,
It clicks.

There is this little section in your brain,
It separates the two states-
> Good and bad, evil and virtuous.

I think,
You're the one to truly determine which path you
cross.

I think that being good
Isn't the default.

> One day,

Sounds are sharper,
Sights are brighter,
Tastes are tangier.

I think,
The default is learning.

Learning until you too
Hear that little click,

Or not.

I'm the Brain

When it comes to the heart and brain,
The heart is the more reckless
and uncontrollable of the two.

On the other hand,
The brain is safe and logical,
Its goal is to just protect itself and the body.

The brain and heart work in tandem
with one another.

Where one lacks,
The other makes up

In due time.

(im)perfect
Not everything is a masterpiece.
But most things are enough t'
get you by with a smile.

Wanting and Needing

I want it back.

I want my tears,
my screams,
I want my love back.

I want you to feel
what I've felt.

I want you to feel what I'm feeling.

I want you to dwell in this inferno
that I've been inside my entire life.

I want the nights you took from me.

I want to wash away the thoughts
of your lying lips.

I want it all gone,
I need you gone.

For good.

Synchronise

My heart is heavy
            but my mind is clear.

                    Maybe one day
            they will each beat unitedly.

one day.

Moments Waiting

For a moment I felt heard
I felt seen.

For a moment,
                    I felt safe.

For a moment I was me.

Now,
Now I've been chipped away.
Broken into forever non-connectable pieces,
Pieces of something that used to be seen as whole.

I've been reduced to nothing but ash,
Ground to null,
just aftereffects of a torturous fire.

So what now you might ask?
    What shall I do with this nothing I'm left with?

This moment I am now living in,
All moments going forward seem to heed the same
result.

                    Nothing.

These life moments now consists of nothingness,

They aren't filled with joy,
My happy glass is empty,
Void of the contentedness I long for.

So again you might ask,
what exactly shall I do now with these nothing
filled moments?

I'm still waiting.

Arbitrary

Sometimes
I get tired of lying.

But the lies still fall

just the same.

Never Good

I'm scared
that if I try,
Truly try
my hardest,
It still won't
amount to anything.

I'm scared
That I still won't be

good enough.
That I'll never be

good enough.

A Week Since

It's been a week since I've died.

A week since you last saw me smile,
The last you held my hand,
The last you heard me laugh.

It's been a week since I've lived.

A week since I splashed in the pool,
Eaten two whole bowls of cereal,
Skipped rocks on the sea shore.

It's been a while
Since I've
Seen you

It hurts,
I know it does,

It truly hurts.

I miss you.
If you can really believe that.

Because without you,
Without me

It's all so hard.
That tether we had
Has broken.

And what's left,
Are fraying strings,

Miles upon miles
Separating us.

I'm gone,

and I'm sorry-

Silent Cry

No one wants to cry forever,

but acting as if you don't want to
doesn't make it go away.

Forever seems to be insistent
On making weeping an inevitability

Truth

Who the hell are you
to tell me
that what i'm feeling
isn't happiness?

Cherry Picking

The shine in your eyes
used to bring me such joy.

The tone in your voice,
it's the sickeningly sweet sap
that traps me.

You have this intoxicating persona
and I can never wait for my next fix.

You look at me like a freshly washed cherry.

I can feel your red stained lips
just barely make contact
with the ripeness of my skin.

To you

i'm just a flavour for you to taste,
something for you to enjoy for a little while.
You snap off my stem
and your teeth pick at my seed.

What's left of me is nothing,
just bits to be thrown away.

And then you gather a handful
of new unsuspecting souls
that are just barely clinging onto life
while you suck what's left out of them too.

Ghostly

Fearing the dark is instinctual.
It's a feral honest assumption
that darkness holds only
the most unpleasant sensations.

Fear of the unknown
is a natural response.

The dark holds unexpected things.

Whether those things turn out to be joys or not,

Fearing the dark is built into our nature.
It is something we use to survive
things we do not recognize.

So yes, I do fear the dark-
You too would fear it
if you were left alone
with it by your side.

Darkness has this everlasting hold on me,
my fear of it sinks me deeper
into its grip.

Love

And the only thing left

is you,
My carnations.

Boom!

Bright lights dancing to the sounding sirens

My nose catches the smell of burnt tire tracks and
kerosene

Hands shaking to the rhythm of my rapid heartbeat
       Head aching, in tune to the pounding on my
            windshield

Still in a daze, eyes thickened; filled with smoke

Crashing sounds fill my body
The rapidness of its movements makes its way

       I sense a calming

I could see the lights glow bright

           I am at the end
           of my journey

The fog lightens up
I can see many yellow suns appear

They then fall back into nothingness

A red beam of heat roars on the hood of my grand
chariot

It grows large, engulfs me

Metal starts screeching

Glass shattering into a thousand knives

My head turns to my back seat
I smile at the sight

My ears stop its eternal ringing

Silence, but then I hear it;

Boom!

Still Wanting

I never asked for much.
I just wanted a bit of attention.
Maybe a smile in my direction,
A splash of love even.

I never asked you to buy me the stars
Or to hang the sun.

Don't act like I asked you to gift me the moon,
Or bottle up the ocean.

I only asked for you to see me,
Listen to me once in a while.
All I asked was for you to love me.

Just love all of me

please.

Origin story

I am not the villain you think I am,
the evil traitor you make me out to be,
the monstrous being put here to test you.

I am no beast,
            no wolf in the shadows.

I do not hide under children's beds
or spook them in their nightmares.

I'm the saviour,
            the hero in this trilogy.

You sit there
            Afraid of your own thoughts
Afraid of the actions you put forth into the world.

I'm free,
Blissfully dancing in your jealousy.

It's what I deserve.

Ignite

The air painted with nips of lavender-vanilla
The sweet scent mixes with the salty drops of love

Champaign covered sheets soaked in bliss
High Rise windows overlooking the night plastered
city

Sweltering with our lasting affection

Her touch, like flames dancing in the wind
Her breath on my flushed skin

A refreshing summer breeze

Her voice, like the sounds of gold covered roses

My lips present blood red and plump

Our necks wear animalistic marks of ownership
My wrists happily taut the burns of velvet rope
Pulling the strings of my desire filled heart

Our flesh, flush against one another,

These bodies forever connected

Lustful pupils blown, swirling with purple and
golden flecks

Her caressing fingertips ignites a fire in me
Burning my core till my insides spill

A rushing sound, as though a waterfall
On this starlit night we commemorate our hearts as
one
A kiss she lays on my swollen lips

Hands tangled in hair

Soft sounds flow sweetly through one another's ears

Hips smashing.
Breathes catching
Eyes meeting.
Lovemaking.
Magically sinful

Standing by

In this world,
Where evil is separated
From good,

Love from
Hatred,

Desire from
Disgust,

All of these feelings,

They are nothing without
One another.

There is a fine balance between opposites,
A balance that mustn't be disrupted.

What would anything be if without
the reference of what good and evil is
to each other.

Joyful Moments

Is it crazy that I find my scars beautiful?

Is it crazy that
      I think back on
            the days where
                  breathing is hard-
                        sounds are too sharp,
                  the light too bright,

                            and I smile?

Is it crazy that these scars
seem to be the only thing
I'm capable of loving.

        They are the only things
that have ever stayed.

END

Sensability

Mortality

There is only one thing that remains contestant in
this world,
And that is the actual end of life itself.

Our mortality is definite,

The only thing that seems to be giving life its
meaning
is the knowledge of that impending end.

The thing that makes you want to live the most,
The thing that stops and makes you think about
what greatness you can leave in your footsteps,

                  That,
that is the knowledge of death.

You wanting to live only because you would rather
not find the end.

It is that knowledge,
that unforeseeable future,
that unknown,

That is what pushes you towards life.

Ironic that we don't even know if death is actually
the end.

Maybe it's the beginning of truly living.

Written by: Alexei